Californians *Who* Made *a* Difference

Heather L. Osial, M.A.Ed.

Consultants

Kristina Jovin, M.A.T.
Alvord Unified School District
Teacher of the Year

Bijan Kazerooni, M.A.
Department of History
Chapman University

Publishing Credits

Rachelle Cracchiolo, M.S.Ed., *Publisher*
Conni Medina, M.A.Ed., *Managing Editor*
Emily R. Smith, M.A.Ed., *Series Developer*
June Kikuchi, *Content Director*
Marc Pioch, M.A.Ed., and Susan Daddis, M.A.Ed., *Editors*
Courtney Roberson, *Senior Graphic Designer*

Image Credits: Cover and p.1 (foreground) Tim Graham/Evening Standard/Getty Images; Cover and pp.1 (background), 21 NASA; pp.2–3 Library of Congress [LC-DIG-fsa-8b32993]; p.6 Ted Streshinsky/CORBIS/Corbis via Getty Images; p.7 Ted Streshinsky/CORBIS/Corbis via Getty Images; p.8 Court Mast/AP Images; p.9 Bettmann/Getty Images; p.10 Walter P. Reuther Library, Archives of Labor and Urban Affairs, Wayne State University; p.11 Farmworker Movement Documentation Project, UC San Diego Library; p.12 George Rose/Getty Images; p.13 Library of Congress [LC-USZ62-52000]; pp.14, 14–15, 29 (bottom) Granger, NYC; p.15, 32 Library of Congress [LC-DIG-ppmsca-50236]; pp.16–17 United Archives GmbH/Alamy Stock Photo; p.17 James Leynse/Corbis via Getty Images; p.19 (foreground) Joker/Martin Magunia/ullstein bild via Getty Images; pp.20, 23, 29 (top) Bettmann/Getty Images; p.22, 31 Reagan Library; p.12 (inset) Silver Screen Collection/Getty Images; pp.24 (left), back cover U.S. Department of Defense; p.24 (right) Fotosearch/Getty Images; p.27 (top) Paul Harris/Getty Images; p.29 (middle) Cathy Murphy/Getty Images; all other images from iStock and/or Shutterstock.

Library of Congress Cataloging-in-Publication Data
Names: Osial, Heather L., author.
Title: Californians who made a difference / Heather L. Osial.
Description: Huntington Beach, CA : Teacher Created Materials, [2018] | Includes index. | Audience: Grades 4-6.
Identifiers: LCCN 2017014115 (print) | LCCN 2017015236 (ebook) | ISBN 9781425854997 (eBook) | ISBN 9781425832476 (pbk.)
Subjects: LCSH: California--Biography--Juvenile literature. | Reformers--California--Biography--Juvenile literature.
Classification: LCC CT225 (ebook) | LCC CT225 .O75 2018 (print) | DDC 920.009794--dc23
LC record available at https://lccn.loc.gov/2017014115

Teacher Created Materials
5301 Oceanus Drive
Huntington Beach, CA 92649-1030
http://www.tcmpub.com
ISBN 978-1-4258-3247-6
© 2018 Teacher Created Materials, Inc.
Made in China
Nordica.072017.CA21700833

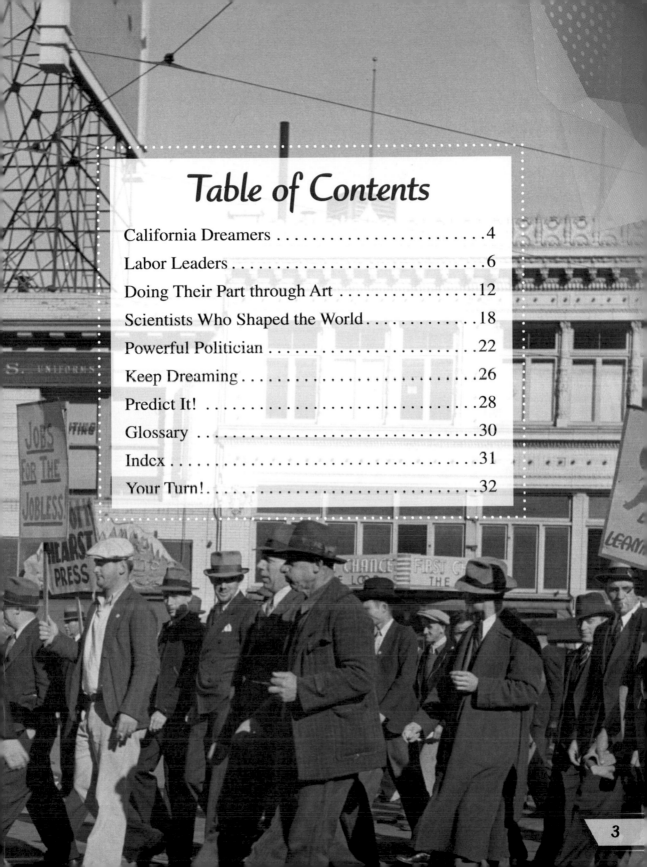

Table of Contents

California Dreamers

California is home to people who work hard to make the world a better place. Their strength inspires others to look for ways to make changes, too. Luckily for them, the state has produced many leaders and dreamers before them. People can look up to and learn from these heroes.

California's past is full of some of the world's best leaders. **Activists** fought to make sure everyone was treated the same. Artists showed the beauty of the country to the world. Scientists taught the power of discovery. And politicians led the nation through some of its hardest times.

These people have shown the impact that one person can have. They have shaped how others live.

California Dreamin'

"California Dreamin'" is one of the most famous songs written about the state. The Mamas and the Papas wrote it while they lived in New York. The song is about the band moving to California to live out their dreams. Even though it is over 50 years old, the song is still loved today.

Diversity

California is one of the most **diverse** states. It is home to more than 10 million people who were born in other countries. And half the children who live in the state have at least one **immigrant** parent. The next generation of difference makers will help move the state forward.

Golden Gate Bridge

Labor Leaders

Today, California leads the way in fair labor laws. But it did not used to be that way. It took people like Cesar Chavez (SEE-sahr SHA-vehz), Dolores Huerta (deh-LOHR-ehs WAHR-tah), and Larry Itliong (IHT-lee-awng) to fight against what they knew was wrong.

Chavez for Change

Cesar Chavez was born in 1927. When he was a child, his family lost their home. They moved to California to find work. They worked on farms around the state. Chavez quit school after eighth grade to work full-time as a farm worker.

Chavez learned first hand the poor conditions and treatment of farm workers. He fought to improve their lives. He stood up for what was right even when it was hard to do. He went on hunger **strikes** and led peaceful marches. His **boycotts** brought workers together in large numbers. For the rest of his life, he fought for equal rights.

Chavez died in 1993. People around the world mourned the loss of a great leader. Tens of thousands of people showed up at his funeral to honor him one last time.

Don't Move

Chavez joined the U.S. Navy during World War II. Days before he was supposed to ship off to serve in the war, Chavez was arrested. He had sat in a "whites only" section of a movie theater. The police were called, but he still refused to move. Chavez did not believe in **segregation** and wanted to take a stand for what he believed in.

Civics

Keep Moving

In 1966, Chavez and 77 others joined a 300-mile (480-kilometer) march. When they reached the end, in Sacramento, they were met by 10,000 people. They wanted to join the cause, too. Those people were a welcome sight to Chavez.

Civics

Chavez had many supporters as he fought for workers' rights.

Teacher and Activist

Dolores Huerta also fought for workers' rights. Her fight began after she graduated from Stockton College. She started working as a teacher. Every day, she saw the barefoot children of farm workers come into her class. They were hungry and tired. Huerta thought it was up to her to help these families. She left teaching and began her life as an activist.

In the late 1950s, Huerta met Chavez. They agreed on many things. In 1962, the two formed the National Farm Workers Association (NFWA). Huerta and Chavez wanted to improve working conditions for all farm workers. They spoke up to make sure workers had clean water to drink and breaks during the day.

Huerta (center) leads a rally.

Honoring Huerta

The Medal of Freedom is the top honor a **civilian** can receive. In 2012, former President Barack Obama gave Huerta this medal. In her speech, Huerta said that change only happens when people work as one. She said it is up to all of us to fix things we know are wrong.

Civics

Many people treated Huerta poorly because of her ethnicity. Others did not want to listen to her because she was a woman. But she never let that stop her. Huerta kept fighting. She played a key role in earning equal rights for women and farm workers.

Huerta has earned many awards. In 1993, she was added to the National Women's Hall of Fame. Huerta still fights for equal rights.

Rallying Cry

¡Sí, se puede! is Spanish for "Yes, it can be done." This is the **motto** of the United Farm Workers (UFW). In 2008, the saying was used in a new way. When Barack Obama ran for his first term as president, many of his supporters chanted, "Yes, we can!" at his rallies. They thought that he gave a voice to people who felt powerless.

Farm workers rally for higher wages.

Leading the Way

Larry Itliong was 15 when he left his home in the Philippines. He moved around the United States as he **canned** fish and picked lettuce. Soon, he moved to California to pick grapes. From there, he would change the course of history.

After years of low pay and poor working conditions, Itliong knew it was time for a change. In 1965, he planned a strike. Itliong led hundreds of grape workers out of the fields. He asked Chavez to join his strike. Chavez agreed. Across the country, people saw what the grape workers were doing. Millions of people stopped buying grapes. After five years, Itliong and Chavez won. Workers received better pay, health benefits, and safer working conditions.

After the grape strike, the two men and Huerta formed the UFW. This group still fights for equal rights.

"Seven Fingers"

While working in Alaska, Itliong earned a new nickname—"Seven Fingers." It came about after he chopped off three of his fingers while canning fish. He had been forced to work in dangerous conditions. Itliong knew he had to force change. He formed a union, which fought for a safer workplace. People soon saw Itliong as someone who would not back down from a fight.

Philippines

United States

Rise to the Top

When Itliong came to the United States, things were very different from his country. He had never lived in a home with electricity before. He had never even slept in a bed! Itliong was in a state of culture shock. But, he soon learned to speak four languages. He watched trials to learn U.S. law. Itliong used these skills to organize workers and fight for equality.

HUELGA

UNITE WITH US

HUELGA

HUELGA

People hold signs that say "strike" in Spanish to urge grape workers to stop working.

Doing Their Part through Art

In California, art and artists have always thrived. Ansel Adams showed the beauty of nature. Dorothea Lange and Amy Tan told the truth, even when it was not what people wanted to see. They helped to shape the state's art culture.

A Voice for the Wild

Ansel Adams began taking pictures at a young age. He did not fit in at school. Adams found it tough to learn and make friends. Instead, he found joy from long walks in nature. On those walks, he took many pictures.

As Adams grew older, he saw the threat that many natural sites were facing. He thought if people could see the beauty that he saw, they would help him save it. Adams became famous for his pictures of Yosemite National Park. The photos were featured in galleries and museums around the world. His work helped save thousands of acres of land that would have otherwise been destroyed.

Adams took many amazing photographs in Yosemite National Park.

Muir's Prophecy

In 1892, John Muir formed the Sierra Club. The club focuses on protecting nature. Years later, he went to Yosemite. Caught by its beauty, Muir cried, "Won't it be wonderful when a million people can see what we are seeing here today?" Muir would turn out to be right. Today, Yosemite welcomes about four million guests per year.

Geography

The Truth of the Lens

Dorothea Lange lived in San Francisco when the Great Depression hit. Before that, she had a nice life. As a young girl, Lange traveled the world. She paid for her trip by selling her photos. But now, poor, hungry people surrounded her.

Lange started taking photos of struggling families. She thought her photos might be able to help them. Her photos soon made her famous. In 1936, Lange snapped a photo of a family. She named it *Migrant Mother*. It would become her most famous work. It shows a mother and her three hungry children. The destruction of the Great Depression is evident in this picture.

When Lange died in 1965, people mourned the loss of a great woman. Her photos let the world see the ugly truths around them. Today, people call Lange one of the best **documentary** photographers of all time.

Dorothea Lange

Health Issues

When Lange was seven years old, she **contracted** polio. Polio is a disease that causes a person's muscles to waste away. While Lange eventually got her strength and health back, the disease left her right leg and foot weak. Walking for a long time was hard for Lange, but she did not let it slow her down. She once said, "[polio] was the most important thing that happened to me."

Migrant Mother

Capturing Heartbreak

The Great Depression began in 1929. Many Americans were left without jobs, homes, or food. At its worst, one out of five people was unemployed. Soup and breadlines formed in major cities because people could not afford their next meals. Lange captured tragic scenes like these for the world to see.

Economics

In 1993, Amy Tan's novel *The Joy Luck Club* was made into a movie.

Poetry Tells the Story

Mai Der Vang is a poet. She was born in the Central Valley. She studied at the University of California, Berkeley. Her poems tell about the lives of Hmong people as they are forced to flee their homeland in Southeast Asia as **refugees**.

A Clash of Customs

Amy Tan was born in Oakland. She is the daughter of Chinese immigrants. Her mother thought Tan should embrace her Chinese **heritage**. But Tan wanted to practice American customs, not Chinese. Tan clashed with her mother for much of her childhood. As a result, they had a tense relationship for many years.

In 1987, Tan and her mother visited China. While there, she met her two half sisters. For the first time, Tan felt a deep connection to her Chinese heritage. When she got home from the trip, she wrote about how she felt. Those thoughts became her first novel. *The Joy Luck Club* was an instant best seller. Tan's words inspired other immigrant children to embrace their families' cultures.

Living with Lyme

In 1999, Tan contracted **Lyme disease**. Unfortunately, doctors did not diagnose Tan for four years. By that time, the illness left Tan with many side effects. While her Lyme disease was never cured, Tan still says she is in "excellent" shape.

Scientists Who Shaped the World

Sergey Brin and Sally Ride are scientists. But while Brin collected data on Earth, Ride did the same thing far above it. Their stories show how Californians have used science to change the world (and beyond).

Brin's Long Journey

Sergey Brin was six years old when his family left Russia. They were Jewish and were harassed for their beliefs. Brin first lived in Maryland, but he moved to California to attend Stanford University. He met a man named Larry Page at school.

Brin and Page wanted to organize all the world's information. Using their math and science skills, they built their first website in 1996. At first, only Stanford students used the search engine. Soon, Brin and Page noticed that people around the world were going to their website. They quickly chose a name. They named their search engine *Google*®.

Naming Google

A *googol* is a math term that stands for the numeral 1 followed by 100 zeroes. Brin and Page thought that was a perfect name for their website. It seemed to them that there was a **vast** amount of information for them to organize.

Larry Page

Sergey Brin

Don't Be Evil

Google's first company motto was Don't Be Evil. Brin and Page thought many companies were taking advantage of people. They wanted Google to be different. In 2015, Google changed its motto. It is now Do the Right Thing.

Sally's Significant Ride

Sally Ride was born in Encino. When she was in college, an advertisement from NASA caught her eye. It said NASA was looking for women astronauts. Ride had always liked math and science. But she had never thought about going to space before. Ride decided to apply for the job. After beating out hundreds of other women, Ride was chosen to go to space.

Ride trained for her trip to space for six years. Then, on June 18, 1983, she boarded a space shuttle and was off! Ride was the first American woman to fly in space. After six days, she and the rest of the crew returned to Earth.

Ride went to space again four months later. After that, she took a job as the director of the California Space Institute. Ride died in 2012, but she will be remembered as the woman who broke the space **frontier**.

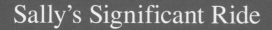

Recognition for Ride

Ride earned many awards. She was inducted into both the National Women's Hall of Fame and the Astronaut Hall of Fame. Ride earned the NASA Space Flight Medal twice. She received the Medal of Freedom (shown here) after her death.

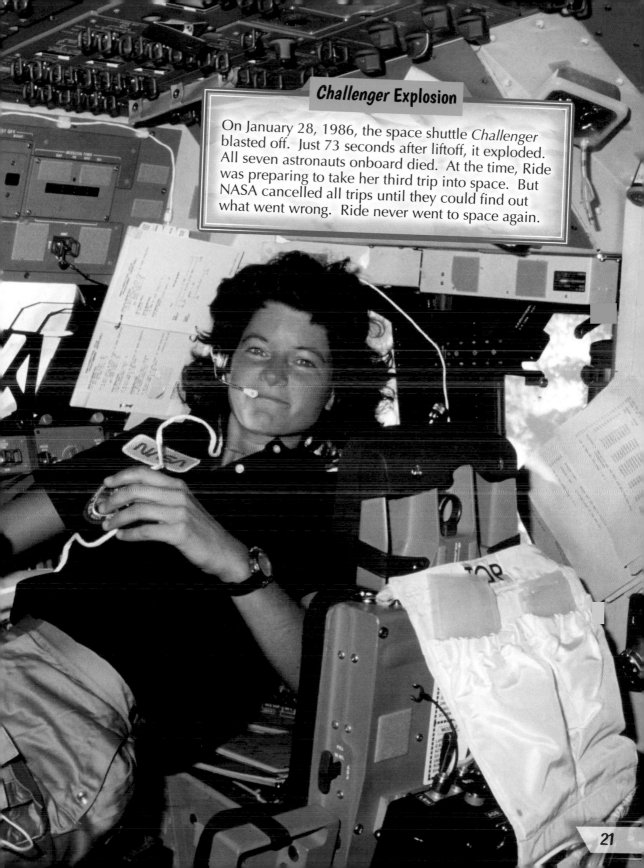

Challenger Explosion

On January 28, 1986, the space shuttle *Challenger* blasted off. Just 73 seconds after liftoff, it exploded. All seven astronauts onboard died. At the time, Ride was preparing to take her third trip into space. But NASA cancelled all trips until they could find out what went wrong. Ride never went to space again.

Powerful Politician

Ronald Reagan was known for his charm and personality. It served him well as an actor. After his acting days were over, he used these traits to lead the state and the country.

Impact on Hollywood

Reagan moved to California in 1937. He hoped to be the next big star. Lucky for him, Warner Brothers needed an actor for an upcoming film. He made his film **debut** in the movie *Love Is on the Air*. From there, he was in over 50 other films. Reagan did not stop with Hollywood, though. In World War II, while in the army, he could not serve in combat because his eyesight was bad. Instead, he made films for the military. Twice, he was president of the Screen Actors **Guild**. He also hosted the TV show *The General Electric Theater* for eight years. It was then that he learned how to be a great public speaker. This skill helped him move from acting to politics.

A Real Hero

Reagan was a lifeguard as a teenager. He worked at a park on a river. In six summers there, he saved 77 people from drowning!

"ROCK"...GREAT COACH, GREAT AMERICAN...GREAT GUY!

KNUTE ROCKNE ALL AMERICAN

WITH
PAT O'BRIEN
GALE PAGE · RONALD REAGAN
DONALD CRISP
Directed by LLOYD BACON

Win One for the Gipper

In the movie, *Knute Rockne, All American*, Reagan played the role of a football player who becomes sick. Right before he dies in the movie, he says, "Go out and win one for the Gipper." Reagan's skill in that scene earned him a lot of praise.

Governor

Reagan registered as a **Republican** in 1962. For the next few years, he traveled the country. He gave speeches and campaigned for his party's candidates. Then, in 1966, he ran for governor of California and won. He worked hard to cut spending. When he ran for reelection, he won again. During his second term, he worked on the **welfare system**. After that, Reagan toured the country again. He spoke to people about what they would like to see fixed. And he set his sights on a bigger role in politics.

Ronald Reagan

REAGAN~BUSH in '80
Let's Make America Great Again

President

In 1981, Reagan was elected the 40th president. When he took office, the U.S. **economy** was not doing well. His first task was to help fix it. He used budget cuts and tax cuts to do this. He ran again and won in a **landslide**. During his second term, he worked to end the **Cold War**. Reagan left office as one of the most popular presidents to ever serve.

Ronald Reagan Presidential Library and Museum in Simi Valley

Dalip Singh Saund

In 1957, Dalip Singh Saund was elected to the U.S. Congress. He was the first congressman born in Asia. Saund was born in a small village in India. He came to the United States in 1920 to study at UC Berkeley. Saund was also the first person elected to Congress who practiced the Sikh religion.

Keep Dreaming

California is home to activists and artists. Scientists and politicians have found their places in the state, too. Many Californians have made a difference. Some people make small changes. They do things to help their neighbors. Others change the world. And as the state continues to grow, there will be more and more difference makers.

Anyone can make a difference. You do not have to be in a position of power to do so. All you need is the grit and determination to make things better. And you have to believe in yourself and your abilities. So, what can you do to make a difference? It does not have to change the world. You can start small, but keep dreaming big. If you do that, you might just be the next Californian who makes a difference!

Charity Work

Volunteering for a charity is an easy way to make a difference. And California has plenty from which to choose. There are over 90,000 in the state! Some charities fight for clean air or to keep animals safe. Others work to build homes or serve food to the hungry. Think about what needs to change, and start making a difference today.

Civics

Tennis Titan

Venus and Serena Williams learned early in life the effect a person can have. So, Serena started the Serena Williams Fund (SWF). The SWF builds schools, gives scholarships for college, and brings food to people around the world.

Tennis stars Venus (right) and Serena Williams pose with their father. They grew up in Compton.

Predict It!

You have now learned about some great people who have made California awesome. Choose one of the people in this book or find your own example. Create a time line of his or her journey. Start with where he or she was born. Make sure to include key events in the person's life, especially those that transformed California for the better. Finally, reflect on how that person has directly affected you.

Now, track your own time line. Where were you born? Where are you now? Where will you go in the future? Continue your time line with your predictions. We each have our own amazing adventure to tell, and we each play a part in the whole story. What will you give back to California? The sky is the limit.

Glossary

activists—people who use or support strong actions, such as protests, to make changes

boycotts—protests where people agree to not buy, use, or participate in something

canned—cleaned, salted, and placed something in a can to be eaten later

civilian—a person who is not part of the military

Cold War—a conflict between the United States and Soviet Union

contracted—became ill with

debut—a person's first appearance in an acting role

diverse—made up of things that are different from each other

documentary—a type of art form that focuses on people or events

economy—the system of buying and selling goods and services

ethnicity—belonging to a group of people that has common cultural ties

frontier—a boundary

guild—a group of people who have the same interests

heritage—traditions and beliefs that are part of the history of a group or nation

immigrant—referring to a person who comes to a country to live there

landslide—a large number of votes going to one side

Lyme disease—an illness spread by ticks that can cause serious problems if not treated

motto—a slogan identifying a place or thing

refugees—people who leave countries for safety

Republican—a person belonging to one of the two major political parties in the United States

segregation—the practice of separating groups of people based on their race or religion

strikes—periods of time when people refuse to do something to force things to change

vast—very great in size, distance, or amount

welfare system—a way for governments to help people in need